Contents

PART ONE: THE CAUSES OF DIVISIONS

I. Political Disorders That Divide

II. Practices That Divide

The
Causes, Evils, and Cures of
Heart and Church Divisions

Extracted from the
Works of Burroughes and Baxter

By Francis Asbury

Abridged and Updated

Seek peace and go after it.

—Psalm 34:14

✠)Abingdon Press

Nashville

THE CAUSES, EVILS, AND CURES OF HEART AND CHURCH DIVISIONS

Copyright © 2015 by Abingdon Press

Library of Congress Cataloging-in-Publication Data

Names: Asbury, Francis, 1745-1816. | Burroughs, Jeremiah, 1599-1646. Irenicum to the lovers of truth and peace. | Baxter, Richard, 1615-1691. Cure of church-divisions.
Title: The causes, evils, and cures of heart and church divisions / by Francis Asbury.
Description: First [abridged edition]. | Nashville, Tennessee : Abingdon Press, 2016.
Identifiers: LCCN 2015038659 (print) | LCCN 2015039653 (ebook) | ISBN 9781501820786 (binding: adhesive casebound : alk. paper) | ISBN 9781501820793 (e-book)
Subjects: LCSH: Christian life. | Church controversies.
Classification: LCC BV4501.3 .A786 2016 (print) | LCC BV4501.3 (ebook) | DDC 262—dc23
LC record available at http://lccn.loc.gov/2015038659

9781791031251 Paperback Edition, 2023

Scripture quotations are from the Common English Bible. Copyright © 2011 by the Common English Bible. All rights reserved. Used by permission.
www.CommonEnglishBible.com.

The excerpts in this volume are abridged and updated from *The Causes, Evils, and Cures of Heart and Church Divisions*, extracted from the works of Mr. Richard Baxter and Mr. Jeremiah Bur-roughes, Philadelphia: Printed by Parry Hall, no. 149, Chestnut Street, and sold by John Dick-ins, no. 182, in Race Street near Sixth Street, MDCCXCII [1792].

In 1792 Francis Asbury extracted the edition above from two sources: (1) Jeremiah Burroughes, *Irenicum, to the Lovers of Truth and Peace Heart-Divisions Opened in the Causes and Evils of Them: With Cautions That We May Not Be Hurt by Them, and Endeavours to Heal Them* (London: Robert Dawlman, 1653); (2) Richard Baxter (1615–1691), *The Cure of Church-Divisions, or, Directions for Weak Christians to Keep Them from Being Dividers or Troublers of the Church with Some Direc-tions to the Pastors How to Deal with Such Christians* (London: Nevil Symmons, 1670).

Contents

Publisher's Note to the 2016 Edition

As we grapple with differing views about and pre-scriptions for important issues of our day, we seek to live up to our calling as Jesus's disciples. Humbly, we fervently ask, "Are we one with God?" And we remind ourselves that spirited disputes are not new within our Wesleyan family in the ongoing search for authentic faith.

The United Methodist Publishing House is pleased to make available, for at least the third time, a version of *The Causes, Evils, and Cures of Heart and Church Divisions*. The book first appeared in 1792. It was an edited volume drawn from two older works (see page ix).

The volume appeared again in 1849. It had been rec-ommended in *The Book of Discipline*; and after The Meth-odist Episcopal Church divided in 1844, the publisher brought this book back into print.

A copy of the 1849 edition was recently found in the rare book room of The United Methodist Publishing House in Nashville, Tennessee, as we prepared to move to a new facility. We quickly concluded that the people called Methodists may find in this historic book, yet again, deep insights of encouragement and instruction as we continue the journey of faith.

By the grace of God, may it be so.

Neil M. Alexander, President and Publisher
Brian K. Milford, Chief Content Officer and Book Editor
R. Carl Frazier, Chair, UMPH Board of Directors
Connie A. Clark, Vice Chair, UMPH Board of Directors

Publisher's Note to the 1849 Edition

The Book of Discipline recommends (Part i, chap. iv, § 16) "a serious perusal of *The Causes, Evils, and Cures of Heart and Church Divisions.*" The work has long been out of print, so that the recommendation could not be complied with. A new edition is now furnished at a low price, with a view to its general circulation. Recent events have tended, perhaps, to weaken the spirit of union among us—it may be well for us to scrutinize our hearts and lives more closely. "If we are united, what can stand before us? If we divide, we will destroy ourselves, the work of God, and the souls of our people."

J. M'Clintock, January 1, 1849

To the Ministers and Members of The Methodist Episcopal Church

Dear Brother and Sisters,

In the course of my reading some years ago, I met with an old book, written by a worthy pastor in the church, Mr. Jeremiah Burroughes, on "Heart Divisions, the Evil of our Times." Feeling at that time the pain of a partial separation in spirit and practice from some who were as my brethren and sons in the gospel, that book proved as a balm and a blessing to my soul. I saw so clearly the evil consequences of a division, and how good and pleasant a thing it is for brothers and sisters to dwell together in unity, that I began to abridge my obsolete but valuable book and earnestly wished, prayed, and strove for unanimity. Soon after, I met with another old book, entitled *The Cure of Church Divisions*, written by that venerable servant of God, the John Wesley of his day, in wisdom, affection, zeal, and a pacific spirit; I mean Mr. Richard Baxter, of precious memory. Being highly pleased with his evangelical sentiments, I concluded to make an extract from both, not doubting but it might be of great service to the church of Christ. And now I recommend it to all ministers of the gospel, and professing Christians of every denomination, into whose hands it may come, pleading with them to read it carefully and with much prayer that they may cultivate a spirit of unity and brotherly love. I remain, dear brothers and sisters, your servant for Christ's sake,

Francis Asbury, 1792

PART ONE

THE CAUSES
OF DIVISIONS

*Though we cannot think alike, may we not love alike?
May we not be of one heart, though we are not of one
opinion? Without all doubt, we may. Herein all God's
children may unite, notwithstanding these smaller
differences.*

—from a sermon by John Wesley

I. Political Disorders That Divide

◇

1. Pride

A proud person makes his or her will the rule of actions and would have it be the rule of other people's too. And other people being proud would have their wills be the rule of their opponent's actions. Thus the blustering wind of pride in a people's hearts causes them to jostle against each other and so to split themselves one upon another. It's what happens where many ships lie together, a violent wind breaking their anchor-cables, and causes them to dash one upon another and thus to wreck the ships even in the haven.

Now let each person look into his or her own heart and see what pride has been and still is there and be humbled before the Lord for this. All you contentious, contrary, quarrelsome people, you are charged this day from God with being men and women of proud spirits, and what evil there is in our sad divisions, that pride in your chest is a great cause of it. St. Paul said, "I'm landing punches on my own body and subduing it like a slave. I do this to be sure that I myself won't be disqualified after preaching to others" (1 Cor 9:27).

2. Self-Love

Philippians 2:3-4: "Don't do anything for selfish purposes, but with humility think of others as better than yourselves. Instead of each person watching out for their own good, watch out for what is better for others." This is the cause of strife, because people look so much on their own things. Many will have no peace, except their own party be followed. It is not peace but party that they mind. *Maxima pars studiorum est studium partium*; that is, the greatest part of their studies is to study sides and parties.

Self causes people not to see their own evils, or if they do, to indulge themselves in them. But to be quick-sighted and severe in the discovering and opposing those evils that are in others, and this causes many splits and separations.

There is this wickedness in self-love, that even those things that people acknowledge to be right and good in the general, yet if they won't particularly agree with something they would have, it will put people into opposition. And what peace and union can there be among people, if what they will grant, and commend to be good, yet when it falls into their laps, they will oppose and contend against it?

Self causes people not to see their own evils or, if they do, to indulge themselves in them.

3. Envy

Envy is a squint-eyed fool. Sometimes you see persons seeking to rake and gather together all they can of any mistakes, political disorders, or miscarriages, by hearsay, letters, or any way, so that by it they may fill up their dung-cart. They lay aside the good, the grace or gifts of God in people—those are laid aside or passed slightingly over, and if at all mentioned—and it is mingled with some dirt. Surely this is an envious person, outfitted for strife and debate, whom God permits to be an affliction to God's people in raising up a spirit of strife and contention and causing divisions among them.

The Holy Spirit says that envy is rottenness to the bones. This vile sin has caused a rot in many persons of eminent abilities and places who might otherwise have done much service for God and God's people in church and state. Oh it is a mischievous sin! "Take away envy," says Augustine, "and what you have is mine; take away envy, and what I have is yours."

4. Passion

Those people who, upon every trifle, are all on fire by their passions and what lies within them set others on fire. They exceedingly disturb the peace of those places where they live and those societies of which they are members. Their hot passions cause the climate where they live to be like the Torrid Zone, too hot for any to live near them. Christ is the Prince of Peace, and the devil is the prince of division. Ephesians 4:26-27: "Don't let the sun set on your anger. Don't provide an opportunity for the devil." You are loathe to give way to your brother or sister. You will say, "What, will I yield to them?" You won't yield to them, but you will yield to them what is worse—to the devil. So you do when you yield to wrath.

Our hearts have been broken one from another in our unhappy divisions. Oh that they could break one toward another in love and tenderness! Here would be a sacrifice more esteemed of God than thousands of rams and ten thousand rivers of oil: to "embrace faithful love and walk humbly" (Mic 6:8).

5. Rigidness

Rigid, harsh, sour, crabbed, rough-hewn spirits are unfit for union. There is no sweetness, no amiableness, no pleasantness in them. They please themselves in a rigid austereness but are pleasing to none else. In their ways, they will abate nothing of their own views nor yield anything to others. This is against the rule of the apostle: "Each of us should please our neighbors for their good in order to build them up. Christ didn't please himself, but, as it is written, *The insults of those who insulted you fell on me*" (Rom 15:2-3).

This is the duty not of weak people only, who have a need to please others because they have need of them. Those who are strong ought not to please themselves but seek to please others. People who are of austere spirits, affecting gravity that turns to a dull, sullen sternness, think this commends the strength of their spirits, that they can carry themselves as they do toward others, altogether content with themselves, without any yielding to others.

6. Rashness

Rashness causes people suddenly to provoke others without considering what ill consequences might come of it. Rash people quickly take hold of the sword of justice to hack and hew. They think that what they do is according to reason, but they don't wisely weigh things in the balance of justice. Remember, justice has a balance as well as a sword. Proverbs 29:11: "Fools show all their anger." Rash fools, by uttering all their anger, suddenly cause great stir and trouble wherever they go. The Hebrew word that signifies a fool, and that which signifies suddenly, rashly, is from the same root.

When peace sometimes is even concluded and there is great joy in hopes of a comfortable agreement, rashness will suddenly break it, without any due consideration.

7. Willfulness

In most people, will is the axle; lusts and passions are the wheels, whereupon almost all their actions are carried. Where there is much will, though the thing be little about which people contend, the opposition may still be great, as if a little stone is thrown with a strong arm, which may make a deep impression.

It is a dangerous thing to have a people's wills engage in matters of difference. It is easier to deal with the reason of twenty persons than with one person's will. A person of a willful, stout spirit stands as a stake in the midst of a stream. What hope can there be of union, where there will be no yielding?

Many times stubbornness comes from weakness rather than strength. There is not always the greatest strength of judgment where there is the greatest strength of will. The dullest horses are not always the most easily reined. Many people are persuaded before they know; those who are persuaded before they know won't be persuaded to know.

8. Inconstancy

Inconstancy is evil and a cause of division. Stubbornness is evil and a cause of division. A person must not be one thing one day and another on another day. Not like a weathercock, carried up and down with every wind. Neither must a person be willful and stout. Not like a rusty lock that won't be stirred by any key. True constancy and a settled spirit are obtained by much prayer and humiliation before the Lord.

Where true constancy is attained by the Spirit of God, and not by the stubbornness of your own, there is exercised much grace and an increase in grace, as well as faith, humility, love, meekness, and patience.

If a person is resolute and constant in one thing but very fickle and easily turned aside in others, there is cause to suspect that the constancy is from stiffness rather than from grace. Grace works proportionally through the whole being and in the whole course of a person's life.

9. Jealousy

"Jealousy, conflict, verbal abuse, and evil suspicions" (1 Tim 6:4). Conflict and evil suspicion are relatives. If contentious people can get nothing against their brothers and sisters, they will surmise there is something. If they can find nothing in their actions to judge, they will judge their hearts. If there is nothing above-board, they will think there may be something under-board. And from thinking there may be something, they will think it very likely there is something; and from likely there is, they will conclude "surely there is some plot working." But this is against the law of love, because love "doesn't keep a record of complaints" (1 Cor 13:5). All the good that they see in their brothers and sisters is blasted by their suspicion of evil.

10. Contention

Some people have a vehement, strong disposition in their hearts for contention. They are like salamanders, which love and live in the fire. They thirst after the waters of Massah and Meribah. Their temper is such as if they drank no other drink than what was brewed of those waters—contentions and controversy.

What is as tedious to other people as death, contention is their delight. They are most in their element when their head and ears overflow with contention. A contentious spirit will always find matters for contention. Proverbs 26:21: "Like adding charcoal to embers or wood to fire, / quarrelsome people kindle strife." They are ready to put their hands into any strife they meet with. Many people have no mettle in anything but contentions. Like many worn out horses that are dull in travel, they have mettle only to kick and to play ill-tempered tricks. If you have any spirit, any zeal and courage, it is a pity it should be laid out in quarrels.

II. Practices That Divide

◇

1. Whispering

Many persons have moderate spirits if left alone. Yet upon meeting other persons who tell them stories, they speak ill of those persons that previously they had a good opinion of, before they have examined what the truth is. A venom got into their spirits. Before they are aware, their hearts begin to be hot and to rise against those people of whom they hear such things. Their thoughts are altered concerning them; their spirits alienated. Breaches are made; and people who are innocent wonder how it all came about. Oh take heed of these people with evil tongues! Saint Augustine couldn't endure such guests at his table, and therefore had the two lines written over his table (and it would be well that they were written over some of your tables):

> *To speak ill of the absent forbear*
> *Or do not sit at table here.*

2. Needless Disputes

When people have a little knowledge, they think it is a fine thing to be arguing and disputing in matters of religion. Unnecessary disputes are their necessary practice, because they will be accounted as nobody if they don't have something to object against almost everything. But in this behavior they hope to be accounted as knowing people, people who have an insight into things, who understand more than ordinary people do. Hence they turn all their religion into disputes, and by them they grow giddy.

Wine is good in its proper place and use, but when it fumes all up into the head, it makes it giddy. Knowledge is good when the strength of it gets to the heart, to comfort it, there to breed a good spirit, for strengthening the heart in the ways of holiness. But when it flies all up into the head, it fills it with thousands of fancies. It causes pride and giddiness. Disputes draw the best spirits from the heart, by which they weaken it. It is a very ill sign in a person to have a contradicting spirit, to get into a vein of disputing against anything, though it be good. "Welcome the person who is weak in faith—but not in order to argue about differences of opinion" (Rom 14:1).

3. Meddling

When people meddle with things that don't concern them, they are out of bounds. "Aim to live quietly, mind your own business" (1 Thess 4:11).

> *It is honorable to back off from a fight,*
> *but fools jump right in.*
> *(Prov 20:3)*

When manna was gathered and kept in that proportion God would have it, it was very good. But when people wanted more and kept it longer than God would have them, then it bred worms. Thus it will be in all that we have or do. Let's keep the proportion God sets before us, and all will be well. But if we think to provide better for ourselves, by going beyond our measure, worms are presently bred in all.

4. Slander

Evil reports may be spread, you know, otherwise than by the tongue; and this is an old divisive practice. If we can blast the chief of a party, we will do well enough with the rest. Therefore let's make as many ill interpretations of what they do as we possibly can. With pretense, let's fasten as many ill or colorful things upon them as we can. Let reports be raised, fomented, and spread—whether they be true or not, it doesn't matter. Something will stick. Let's be able to say we heard it, or there was a letter written about such a thing, and we will boldly assert it. The apprehension of it will prevail with many, so that people don't have the esteem in their hearts that they had previously. And once we suppress their esteem, we will do well enough with their cause.

As for God's servants, they commit their names and ways to God, knowing that the Lord takes care of their names as well as their souls. If dirt is cast upon a mud wall it sticks, but if cast upon marble, it soon washes or crumbles away. God will in time justify his servants, even in your consciences, by the constancy of their peaceable demeanor toward people and their gracious, holy walking with their God.

5. Inordinate Respect

This was the practice among the Corinthians, which caused great divisions among them. Some preferred Paul, some preferred Apollos, some preferred Cephas. Without question, a person may be revered and prized in the heart, and we may outwardly show more respect (than to others), to those whom God makes the greatest instruments of good. But people still should take heed that they give not so much honor to one that they deny due respect to others. And ministers, and others in public places, should not entertain, much less seek for or rejoice in, any honor or respect given to them that they see detracts from that esteem and countenance that are due to others.

The weakness and folly of people in their inordinate giving or denying respect are often caused but more ordinarily fomented and increased by the pride and vanity of teachers who seek respect. This causes parties to form, and more hurt comes to the public than their honors are worth a thousand times over. One person's money in a market is as good as another's; so should one person's reason and truth be as good as another's.

6. Single-Issue Judgments

Some people are of such dividing dispositions that if they are offended with someone in any one thing, in their hearing or otherwise, they will go away in a touchy mood, resolving never to hear more from the person.

You think you have liberty in any contrary mood to reject the good things that God offers to you, to partake of a community's gifts and graces as you please. Perhaps your stomach is suddenly so high and great, or your spirit is fallen into such a sullen sourness, that you won't so much as go or inquire to see if, upon a serious and quiet examination of things, you may not have satisfaction concerning what presently offends.

No person's spirits are sustained with such present, rash, heady resolutions. Not since the Christian religion entered the world has there been the kind of spirit prevailing among those who profess godliness. Never have so many withdrawn from hearing, even among those whom they acknowledge God has spoken to their hearts.

Certainly, if you have no need of the word, the word has no need of you. You may easily express your discontent to each other. You may easily say you are resolved you will never listen to this person anymore. But you cannot so easily answer this to Jesus Christ.

7. Compromising against the Common Good

Some who profess godliness make use of wicked people, commend them, join with them, embrace them, even be well pleased with the bitterness, boisterousness, and boldness of their daring spirits. When they make use of them, against those people and ways they differ from, this is an evil that brings guilt upon themselves, and it makes the division between them and their brothers and sisters very great. If your hearts are right and your cause is good, you need not make use of anything that is evil to comfort your hearts or to maintain your cause. The Lord won't be obligated to the evil bitterness of some party's spirits for the furtherance of God's cause, and why should you? God won't take the wicked by the hand; neither should you. Why do you seek to strengthen yourselves by stirring up vile people to join with you, such as previously your hearts were opposite to? How can it be that you can be so close and loving now? You can smile one upon another and shake hands together. How did that happen, that they encourage you, and you encourage them? Those unsavory, bitter expressions that came from them you now can smile at and be well pleased with because they are against what you oppose. Blow up that sparkle of ingenuity that previously had been in you. Lay your hands upon your hearts, think to yourselves, Is it the Spirit of Jesus Christ that actuates us in this way? Surely this is not the way of peace but of division and confusion.

8. Revenge

When any provoke you, you decide you will get even with them. There is a way whereby you may not get even with them but above them—that is, forgive them. Practicing revenge is the way to continue divisions to the end of the world. So and so offends me, therefore I will offend them, and therefore they offend me again, and I them, and so it may run *ad infinitum*. They deny me a kindness, therefore I will deny them, and therefore they will deny me; so these unkindnesses run on endlessly. Divisions will have a line of succession. Where will it, where can it stop, if this is our way?

A gentleman of very good credit, who lived at court many years, told me that he once heard a great man in the kingdom say he never forgave a man in his life, and I am moved to believe it to be so because I have been told by some other gentlemen that the same man would, when he was walking alone, speak to himself and clap his hands upon his breast, and swear by the name of God that "he would be revenged, he would be revenged."

PART TWO

THE EVILS OF DIVISIONS

What heart, which has any tenderness in it, bleeds not in the sense of these sore and dreadful heart divisions there are among us? The evil there is in them is beyond what tongue or pen can express. Consider: (1) the good they hinder, and (2) the sin they cause.

I. The Good They Hinder

◇

1. They Hinder Quietness, Comfort, and Spiritual Sweetness

Divisions put the spirit out of tune. People who previously had sweet spirits full of ingenuity, since they have interested themselves in these divisions, have lost their sweetness, and their ingenuity is gone. When the bee stings, she leaves her sting behind her and never gathers honey again. People by stinging each other don't lose their stings, but they lose their honey; they are never likely to have that sweetness in their hearts that previously they had.

Your contending costs you dear. Though it were in nothing else, yet the loss of this sweetness of spirit makes it very costly to you. All the wrong that you should have put up if you had not contended, had not been so great an evil to you as this one thing is. There is nothing more contrary to ingenuity than quarrelsomeness.

People seldom come away from hot disputes, or any other contentions, without their spirits altered for the worse. They find it so, and others find it in them.

2. They Hinder Spiritual Freedom

The strength of many people is spent on arguments. They have no command over anything else. When a person is once engaged in a contest, he or she doesn't know how to get away from it. Contention is a great snare to a person. He wishes he had never meddled with it; she is weary of it but knows not how to come out of it fairly.

We read of Moses (Deut 34:7) that he was 120 years old when he died. His eye wasn't dim nor his natural force abated. Some offer one reason for such a wonderful preservation of his health and strength: the meekness of his spirit. God describes him (Num 12:3) as the most humble man upon the face of the earth.

3. They Hinder Sweetness of Communion

You know your communion with the saints desires to be far sweeter than it is now. You prefer to have your hearts spring at the sight of each other: *Ipse aspectus boni viri delectat*, says Seneca. "The very sight of a good person delights." The sight of a godly person once delighted us otherwise than now it does. You look one upon another now sourly, with lowering countenance, and withdraw from one another.

Your comforts once were double, triple, sevenfold, a hundredfold among the society of saints you once conversed with. Oh the sweetness there once was in the spirits of Christians! It was blessed oneness of heart. Oh how did they love to open their hearts to each other! What delight was there in pouring forth their spirits into each other! What cheerfulness was there likely to be in their meeting! They ate their bread together with sincere union and joy, praising the Lord. They parted from each other with their whole beings bound up in each other: their hearts warmed, enlarged, resolved, and strengthened in God's ways. But now they can't meet together without jarring and contending with each other. They part with spirits estranged from, soured, and embittered one against another, their hearts weakened and more unsettled in the things of God than before.

4. They Hinder Our Time

A huge amount of time is spent over our divisions, for which we are not able to give account to God. When people are engaged in contentions, they will follow them night and day—whatever other business might be neglected. Indeed, the choice of our time that might be spent in meditation, reading, and prayer is now spent in contending and arguing. Those retired times when we preferred to converse with God are now spent in the workings of our own thoughts about divisions. And when we move about in public a great part of our time is given up in going first to this body and then to the other, to help forward and foment a matter of division. Of all the time allotted to a person's life, that time spent in legal maneuvers and quarrelling is the worst. Happy it would be for many that it might not be counted among the days, weeks, or months of their lives.

5. They Hinder Our Prayers

"If two of you agree on earth about anything you ask, then my Father who is in heaven will do it for you," says Christ (Matt 18:19). Private contentions in families are a great hindrance to family prayers; so our public divisions and contentions are the great hindrance of the prayers of Christians in a more public way. How Christians desire to pour forth their hearts in prayer together! But now it is otherwise. People don't now walk together as the heirs of life; therefore their prayers are hindered. God does not accept our gift if we offer it when our hearts are at a distance from our brothers and sisters. When splits continue, and we are not reconciled, you know that Christ requires us to leave our gift at the altar until reconciliation is made. It is the Spirit of God in the saints that is the spirit of prayer. Now God's Spirit is like a dove, meek, quiet, and peaceable.

6. They Hinder Use of Our Gifts

When containers are soured with vinegar, they spoil liquor that is poured into them; they make it good for nothing. Many people have excellent gifts, but they are in such sour, vinegar spirits that they are of little or no use in church and commonwealth.

They have no hearts to impart their gifts to their brothers and sisters, in counseling, admonishing, strengthening, and comforting. No, their hearts are estranged from them; they care not to have anything to do with them. But do you think you are so committed to your own group that you may keep in or employ your talents as you please? Are you not the stewards of Christ? Are they not given to you for the edification of your brothers and sisters, as well as for good to yourselves? Can this satisfy your consciences?

If you do make use of your gifts for the good of others, yet dissensions between you will hinder the profit from them. You are not likely to do any good by them. Unless the oil of love carries them through, they won't soak into people's hearts.

7. They Hinder Our Graces

How little of God and Christ, how little spirituality in confessors of religion since these splits and divisions have been among us! Here is the reason for the deadness, coldness, emptiness, barrenness, and spiritual emptiness—you are not joined. Where are the heavenly Christians who once were humble—those holy, gracious souls who lived by faith, who were able to deny themselves? Their whole lives were nothing but a continual exercise of self-denial. Christians who were not only patient but joyful under afflictions? Where are those watchful Christians who walked close with God, who enjoyed such spiritual communion with God that it made their faces shine in their holy, heavenly conversations? Where are those tender, broken-hearted Christians that once lived upon the word, to whom the word was sweeter than honey and the honeycomb?

Our divisions hinder our strength. If you untwist a cable, how weak is it in the several parts of it! A threefold cord is not easily broken, but a single one is. Divide a strong current into several rivulets and how shallow and weak will the course of the water be! They hinder our doing good in public: that which concerns many must be done by many. But how can two, much less many, walk together, if they are not agreed? That which one does the other seeks to undo.

None are more crossed in their ends and designs than contentious people. We have not the mutual benefit of each other's resources, houses, the many ways of accommodation and help for each other, as previously we had.

II. The Sin They Cause

◇

The number *two* is counted as a cursed number because it was the first that parted from unity. The departure from that unity God would have is very cursed because it has much sin in it. That which Augustine says of original sin we may well apply to our divisions: "They are sin, the punishment of sin, the cause of sin, nothing but a pile of sin."

1. They Violate the Law of Love

Division is against the solemn charge and command of God and of Jesus Christ: "This is his commandment, that we believe in the name of his Son, Jesus Christ, and love each other as he commanded us" (1 John 3:23). It is not an arbitrary thing that we should love each other, but it is the command of God and a great command joined to that of believing in God's Son, Jesus Christ. The one is as truly necessary to salvation as the other. Let people talk of faith, of believing about God's Son, of trusting toward free grace in Christ. Yet if they have dividing, contending spirits, no love, no sweetness, no grace of union with the saints, then their faith is a dead faith. And because God stands so much upon this requirement to have God's people live together in love, at the beginning of the verse the writer says, "This is his commandment," and at the end of the verse the writer says "as he commanded us." It is a gift, because it is a sweet commandment.

2. They Are against the Prayer of Christ

These unkind and unloving divisions are against the prayer of Jesus Christ, indeed, against that prayer he made for us a little before he died. In John 17:21, he prayed to his Father that all who did believe and should after believe in him, that they may be one in the Father and Jesus. As if Jesus should say,

> Father, I am now going out of the world, and I foresee when I am gone, even those whom you have given me, who are one in me and in you, will meet with strong temptations to divide themselves from each other. But, Father, I plead with you, let your fatherly care come over them, to keep their hearts together, that they may be united in the strongest union that is possible for creatures to be united in! Father, let them be one, as you and I are one!

Would we not have deep regret to lose the benefit of that heavenly prayer of Christ for us in John 17? Read it over. See what soul-ravishing excellence there is in it, seeing he has expressly said he intended us who live now in it, as well as those disciples who then lived with him.

3. They Dishonor Christ

Our divisions are very dishonorable to Jesus Christ. It would not be so bad if our divisions darkened our name only. But that which darkens the glory of Jesus Christ should go very near to us.

John 17:21, 23 may be as strong an argument against division as any I know in God's book. Christ, praying to the Father for the union of his saints, uses this argument (Father, please let this be granted) "that the world will believe that you sent me." And again, in verse 23: "So that they will be made perfectly one. Then the world will know that you sent me." If they are not united to each other in love and peace but have a spirit of division ruling among them, what will the world think? Surely that you didn't send me. That I who am their head, their teacher, and Lord never came from you. Because you are wisdom, holiness, and love; and if I had come from you, then those who claim me as theirs, and whom I own as mine, would hold forth in their conversations something of that spirit of holiness, wisdom, and love that there is in you.

Surely any Christian heart ought to tremble at the least thought of having a hand in so great an evil as this.

4. They Grieve God's Spirit

Divisions are sinful because they grieve the Holy Spirit. "Don't make the Holy Spirit of God unhappy—you were sealed by him for the day of redemption" (Eph 4:30). Surely every godly heart will say,

> God forbid that I should do anything to grieve the good Spirit of God. It is the Spirit that enlightened me, that revealed to me the great mysteries of God, of Christ, of eternal life. It is the Spirit that drew my whole being to Jesus Christ; that comforted it with those consolations that are more to me than ten thousand worlds. It is the Spirit that strengthened me, that helps me against temptations, that carries me through difficulties, that enables me to rejoice in adversity. So now will I be guilty of so great a sin as to grieve this blessed Spirit of the Lord? I would rather suffer any grief in the world to my own spirit than be any occasion of grief to that blessed Spirit of God.

So would you like to know what it is like to grieve the Holy Spirit further? Consider what follows in Ephesians 4:31-32: "Put aside all bitterness, losing your temper, anger, shouting, and slander, along with every other evil." And would you do what pleases the Holy Spirit? God knows it would be the greatest joy in the world for me to do the following: "Be kind, compassionate, and forgiving to each other, in the same way God forgave you in Christ."

5. They Offend Our Brothers and Sisters

These divisions grieve and offend our brothers and sisters. This should not be a light matter with us. Christ accounts it a great evil to offend one of his little ones. We may think it a little matter to give offence to some of God's people who are poor and indigent in the world—so long as we feel bold and have the support of great men—too bad for them. But friend, whatever slight thoughts you have about it, Christ thinks it a great matter. You may look upon them as under you; the times may favor you more than them. But what if you give them cause to go to God, to make their laments to God about how you have used them, saying,

> Lord, you know I was for peace to the best of my ability, so far as I was able to see from your word for my guide. But these who previously were brothers and sisters to me are now estranged, and their hearts are embittered. Their words and their attitude are very grievous—all because I can't measure up to their opinions or their ways.

Certainly this would prove very ill to you, so regard it as lightly as you will.

It's not the way of Christians, when they apprehend wrong, to seek to right themselves or others by bitter, provoking expressions. But if their hearts are filled with grief, if they need to vent it, and if quiet debates with their brothers and sisters won't ease them, let them vent by pouring forth their complaints to the Lord.

6. They Stir Up Corruption

There is much sin in our divisions because they stir up much corruption on all sides, in ourselves and in others. If you shake a glass of water that has dirt in the bottom, the dirt spreads itself all over, and so in this way we spread the dirty stuff of our hearts. With these divisions causing a commotion, those corruptions are now discovered, which neither ourselves nor others thought had been in us.

Don't say in your hearts, or to each other, Who would have thought it possible that so much filthy stuff should lie so long undiscovered in people's hearts, which now appears since these unhappy divisions have happened among us? James 3:16: "Wherever there is jealousy and selfish ambition, there is disorder and everything that is evil."

When snakes are cold, they lie still; but if the heat of fire comes to them, then they hiss and strike with their stings. Thus corruptions blaze by the fire of contention that is kindled among us, until they begin to stir, to act, indeed, to rise very high.

Chrysostom explains that when people's wrath is stirred by arguing, if it continues to heat up until night, as they lie upon their beds, their corruptions will be boiling. They will lay musing and plotting against those that contend with them. Have you not found it so, when the sun was gone down upon your wrath, you could hardly sleep that night?

7. They Become Stubborn in Sin

As they stir up sin, so they become stubborn in sin, as fire hardens the clay into brick. Thus are people's hearts hardened in evil by our divisions. People who previously had tender spirits, whose hearts were ready to relent upon any admonition from a brother or sister, are now stiff, and they stand out sturdily, indeed, behave themselves scornfully. How this fire of contention has baked their lusts, has hardened their hearts!

In Ezekiel 11, God promises to give his people one heart, which should be a heart of flesh. While the hearts of the saints are united, they are tender. But when they divide, they grow hard. This is the reason it is so hard to convince brothers and sisters, having fallen apart, why either of them don't have a sick character. They are angry, and they think they very well should be angry, and all because their hearts are stubborn. Jonah was in a peeved mood, and his heart was hardened with it. Even when God himself comes to convince Jonah, the prophet waits it out, and Jonah will by no means acknowledge himself faulty. No, what Jonah does he will justify, because he does well to be angry.

8. They Keep Others from God's Ways

There is much sin in divisions because they are a means to keep others away from God's ways. If this is their religion, they say, for Christians to quarrel with each other, we will have none of it. When they see this, they will conclude, surely this isn't the way of Christ.

Divisions are a very ill improvement of our zeal and courage. Zeal and courage have such an excellence that it is a thousand pities they should have no other improvement than to raise and maintain quarrels and divisions. The Lord has use for every person's zeal and courage. Reserve them for the Lord, for some notable work that God has for you to do, and don't spend them about matters that come to no good.

Those who have the most zeal and courage have little enough to serve their turn for the service that God requires of them. Must this be spent in unworthy babbling, competition, and quarrelling?

A person's body is in an ill condition, with a sore that is fed by the bodily fluids, leaving less supply for the parts of the body that are to be nourished and maintained. The sore is fed, but the other parts grow lank and feeble. Thus it is with many people's spirits; they are disordered, and then what abilities they have are drawn away to feed those disorders.

PART THREE

The Cures of Divisions

What gracious heart is not cut in pieces with grief for those sore and fearful evils that there are in and come from our divisions? And is the heart not cut in pieces again with careful thoughts about what may be done to heal divisions?

In Matthew 6:25, Christ forbids that crushing care that cuts our hearts when it comes to matters concerning ourselves, indeed, for our lives. "Don't worry about your life," which means, Don't dwell in thoughts that should cut your hearts in pieces. Why do you divide your hearts? But though this charge of Christ is repeated and repeated again against our careful, dividing, cutting thoughts about ourselves, for uniting the hearts of the saints together, for the good of the church, this heart-cutting care is not only allowed but required, "so that there won't be division in the body and so the parts might have mutual concern for each other" (1 Cor 12:25). To repeat: "so the parts might have mutual concern for each other."

I. Joining Principles

◇

1. Peace and Love Will Reconcile Differences

In the midst of all differences of judgment, and weaknesses of the saints, it is not impossible that we may live in peace and love together.

If there may be peace and love between God and his saints, then surely, notwithstanding these things, the saints may be at love and peace among themselves. Let this groundwork be laid, and let our hearts be very possessed by it. Banish the vain conceit that has disturbed greatly churches in all ages. If people differ in their judgment and practice in matters of religion—though it is in things that are but the weaknesses of godly people, and if there still needs to be flaming hearts and division—let all peaceable people deny this consequence. Let's not say, "it will be so"; and that our words may be made good, afterward, to indeed make it so.

We labored to get our opinions into one, but they won't come together. Perhaps in our endeavors toward agreement we began at the wrong end. Let's try what we can do at the other end; perhaps we will have better success there. Let's labor to join our hearts, to engage our affections one to another. If we can't be of one mind that we may agree, let's agree that we may be of one mind.

2. Strife Won't Gain What Love Can

Strife will never gain what may be had by love and peace. We are all inclined to have our own way. The first thing many people do, if their wills are crossed, is presently to strive and contend. But this should be the last thing, after all other means are tried, and should never be made use of but in case of pure necessity. We should first think, Is there any way in the world whereby it is possible we may have our desires satisfied with peace? Let's try this, and another way, a third, a fourth, indeed, a hundred ways, if they lie between us and the way of strife, before we come to meddle with that.

The way of love, of engaging hearts one to another, is the only way to bring persons into unity of judgment; indeed, the only way when all is done for people to have their wills. I may give you this or the other rule to bring you to think and do the same thing. But the most excellent way, with hyperbole, is the way of love. If you could get your minds to agree by other ways, certainly you could not enjoy it with that sweetness and comfort as you may if you get it this way. Certainly there is no person living who does not repent that he or she ever got their way by strife and contention when it might have been obtained by love and peace.

3. Better to Do Good Than Receive Good

Active good is better than passive. Only God himself, his angels, and saints do good, but all creatures can receive good. This principle would quickly join us, because if this were in a people's hearts, they would study how to do all the good they could to each other. The more good we do to any, the more will our hearts be inclined to love them. The very communication of goodness, if it emerges from a good spirit, carries the heart along with it to the subject this good is communicated to. The more good God does to any, the more God loves them. So it is with us in our share. If you take a poor child from the garbage dump or out of the orphanage and make her your heir, you do not only this good to her because you love her, but you love more because you look upon her as an object of your goodness, as one raised by you.

4. Another Person's Good Is Ours as Well as Theirs

We are all of one body. Whatever good others have, it is the good of the body. It makes them in some way able to do that good that we should have done or at least that we should desire to have done.

If you are godly, you have an interest in all the eminently godly people in the world: in all their gifts, in all their graces, and in all they have or do. All that is in the world that has any good in it is yours. Indeed, what is evil will be serviceable to you for good. All the excellence there is in others is the good of every one of you. A special reason why people contend so much is that they think the good that other people have is their evil; therefore they must either obtain it for themselves or darken it in those that have it. But such people who act out this principle are poor, low-spirited people. A person of an elevated, enlarged spirit opens his or her heart that it may be filled with that infinite good in which there is all good. My whole being then will rejoice in all the good I see my brothers and sisters have and in all they do. I will bless God for it and seek to further what I can.

5. Our Good Is More in the Public Than Ourselves

It is because we have such private spirits that there are such disagreements among us. If we were more transparent, our contentions would vanish. When I read about how open are some believers in other religions, I am ashamed to look upon many Christians. Paulus Emilius, upon hearing of the death of his children, spoke with undaunted courage "that the gods had heard his prayer, which was that calamities should rather happen to his family than to the commonwealth." The public openness of his spirit made it very sweet and lovely. According to the story, he pleaded with his enemies gently and graciously after he had subdued them, setting forward their causes, even as if they had been his confederates, friends, and close relatives. Public-spirited people have sweet and peaceable spirits.

6. The Golden Rule

What I would have others do to me, that I will endeavor to do to them. Wouldn't I have others bear with me? Then I will bear with them. Would I have others do acts of kindness to me? Then I will do acts of kindness to them. Would I have others live peaceably with me? I will do so with them. This rule of treating others how I want to be treated is a law of justice; such justice keeps the peace.

Chrysostom, in his thirteenth sermon to the people of Antioch, makes use of this principle. Thus after Christ had spoken of many blessings, says he,

> Those things you would have others to do to you, do you to them . . . ? Would you receive benefits? Bestow benefits then. Would you have mercy? Be merciful then. Would you be loved? Then love. You should judge yourself as the one who rules your own life. That which you hate, don't do to another. If you can't endure reproach, don't reproach others. If you can't endure envy from others, don't envy others. If you can't endure deception, don't you deceive others.

7. To Yield Is More Honorable Than to Overcome

Many people in their anger will say, I will get even with him. I will tell you a way how you may rise above him: forgive him. By yielding, pardoning, putting up with the wrong, you show you have power over yourself, and this is a greater thing than to have power over another.

If someone offends me merely through weakness, this is their affliction. In this they are neither an enemy to self nor to me. They mourn for it, and I will pity them in their mourning. They are more troubled for what they have done than I have cause to be for what I have suffered. If they offend willingly and purposely, they are their own enemy more than mine.

If, when others wrong you, you don't care what it takes to be right, this is your folly and madness. If someone pricks me with a pin, will I therefore in anger run my knife into my side? If someone is your enemy, will you from one enemy make two? Will you also be an enemy to yourself? Indeed, a greater enemy than any person living can be to you? All the people in the world can't make you sin, except you will it for yourself.

Objection: But how will this join us one to another?

Answer. Very much: both as it holds together the goodness of peace with all people and as it strengthens the heart to make and keep peace with God and one's own conscience. A person who has satisfaction enough within can easily bear affliction and troubles that come from without. This is the cause of the ornery attitude of many men and women in their families and with their neighbors: there are secret gaps between God and their own consciences.

II. Considerations

God is love. There is anger and hatred in God as well as love, but God is never said to be anger or hatred; no, not even justice itself. Rather God prefers to disclose to humans that "God is love."

We Are One

God joined us together as human beings. We are not dogs, not wolves. Then let's not be so to each other. The apostle gives the reason why we must keep the unity of the Spirit in the bond of peace: because "you are one body and one spirit, just as God also called you in one hope. There is one Lord, one faith, one baptism, and one God and Father of all" (Eph 4:4-6). Here you have seven strong reasons to join together for unity.

1. **One body.** The meanest member is in the body. Is it attractive for the body of Christ to be split and torn? What but madness can cause one member to tear and split from another?

2. **One spirit.** "All these things are produced by the one and same Spirit" (1 Cor 12:11). And is not this one Spirit a spirit of love and meekness? What does a contrary, contentious spirit do in you who profess to be a Christian?

3. **One hope.** Are you not heirs, joint heirs, of the same kingdom? And do you contend as if one belonged to the kingdom of light and the other to the kingdom of darkness?

4. **One Lord.** You serve the same Lord and Master. Is it for the credit of a master that his servants are always quarrelling and fighting each other? Is it not a tedious thing in a family that the members can never agree?

5. **One faith.** Even though we don't agree together in some things of lesser importance, we still agree in one faith. Why should we not then keep the unity of the Spirit in the bond of peace? Our agreement in the faith, one would think, should swallow up all the disagreements.

6. **One baptism.** We are baptized into Christ's death. And isn't that to show that we should be dead to all those things in the world that cause strife and contention among people? Our baptism is our badge, our attire.

7. **One God.** Though there be three persons in the divine nature, and every person is God, yet there is but one God. Here is a union infinitely beyond all unions that any creature can be capable of. The mystery of this union is revealed to us to make us in love with union.

III. Directions

◇

1. Value Maturity and Wisdom

Don't forget the great difference between novices and experienced Christians, between the babes and those who are mature, between the weak and the strong in grace. In your estimation, don't put them all on the same level. Some don't listen well, have need of milk, are unskilled in thoughts about righteousness, and must be taught the principles. Others can digest strong meat, who by reason of use, have their senses exercised to discern both good and evil. It is not for nothing that the younger are commanded reverence and submission to the elder and that the pastors and leaders of the church are usually called by the name of elders, because it was supposed that the elder sort are more experienced and wise. Therefore, pastors and leaders are to be chosen out of them.

Therefore remember to give due respect to those who have been longer in Christ than you, to those who have longer studied the scriptures, and to those that have had greater helps and experience.

2. Learn How to Overcome Spiritual Pride

Pride is the self-idolizing sin, the great rebel against God, the chief part of the devil's image, that one sin that breaks every commandment, the heart of the old being, the root and parent and summary of all other sin, the anti-Christian vice that is most directly contrary to the life of Christ. It is called spiritual pride when people are proud of spiritual excellence, real or supposed. And this pride is so much worse than pride in beauty, apparel, riches, high places, or high birth.

Consider that the more you are proud of your goodness, the less you have to be proud of. If this sin is predominant, it is certain that you have no saving grace at all. What an odious thing and miserable case it is to be proud of holiness when you are unholy and to be damned both for the want of it and for being proud of it.

In a word, if God would cure the church of religious pride—the pride of wisdom, the pride of piety and goodness—the church would have fewer heresies and controversies and have much more peace and much more true wisdom and goodness in itself.

3. Don't Act More Holy Than Others

Don't pretend to be eminent and conspicuous in holiness, more than God would allow, by standing at a privileged distance from lesser followers of God. It is a loathsome scab when Christians separate themselves from the rest of the worldly, secular people so that their religion may be a noted thing, and they may be set up in their singularity as public spectacles for the world to admire. One wonders, though, perhaps some conspicuously holy persons come under the grip of conscience, to make amends for the guilt of sexual immorality, murder, or some other notorious sins, which the condemned secular people never committed.

Many people—who perceive how childish a thing it is to set up one's self to be observed for fine clothes, for physical beauty, for elite entertainment, curiosities, houses, lands, or other vanities—still think that it is an excellent thing to be honored by others, especially by the wisest and the best, as a person of wisdom, piety, and goodness. Indeed, it is the truest and highest honor to be wise and good, and it is exceeding natural for a person to desire honor, and it is lawful to have a religious regard for our honor. Though this is true, how easy it is for pride to take this advantage and to go a little farther, while we think we go but thus far and keep within our boundaries.

4. Don't Overvalue Words or Declarations

Don't overvalue the common gift of speech nor an elevated declaration, as if the presence or absence of either proves the presence or absence of grace.

Yet neither of these must be undervalued, nor accounted needless, useless things. But overvaluing them has caused great disorders in the minds and affections, and communion and practice, of many very well-meaning Christians. When God first brought me from among the more ignorant sort of people, and when I first heard religious persons pray spontaneously and speak affectionately and seriously of spiritual and heavenly things, I thought truly that they were all undoubted saints. The sudden apprehension of the difference of their gifts and speech from others made me think confidently that the one sort had the mark of God upon them, and the other had nothing almost of God at all. Until before long, many among those whom I so much honored began to disclose an unscriptural disposition.

5. Carry Each Other's Burdens

Many are so careful to be found exact in their obedience to God that they build up duties and are against sins, based on dark and very far-fetched consequences and upon a few obscure and doubtful passages in scripture, when there are no express words or clear text at all to bear them out. Doubtless, the darkest intimations of God's will must not be disregarded. But, on the other side, we can't encourage them to acknowledge some duties and sins, which are over and over a hundred times more vehemently expressed and argued in the plainest words.

Objection. But those I complain about are guilty of this, that, and the other fault!

Answer. "Brothers and sisters, if a person is caught doing something wrong, you who are spiritual should restore someone like this with a spirit of gentleness. Watch out for yourselves so you won't be tempted too. Carry each other's burdens and so you will fulfill the law of Christ" (Gal 6:1-2), which you think you fulfill by your unwarranted conduct, while you are but fulfilling your selfish passions.

6. Don't Be Governed by Your Passions

Beware of being governed by your passions. We are seldom more mistaken in justifying ourselves than in our passions. When our passions are religious, the mistake is most easy and most perilous. Easy, because we are apt to be most confident and not suspect them, when the matter seems so great and good about which they are exercised. Perilous because the greatness and goodness of the matter makes the error greater and worse. Therefore, remember the difference between true zeal and false: know that one who usually does the right thing, and whose zeal for Christianity is sound, may still have much zeal that is unsound within. It is a bad sign:

1. When your zeal is heightened over some singular opinion that you have owned, and not for the common salvation and substance of the Christian faith or practice; or at least when your peculiar opinion has a greater proportion of your zeal than many more plain and necessary truths.

2. When your zeal is moved by any personal interest of your own, by honor or dishonor; by any wrong that is done to you; or by any reputation for wisdom or goodness that deceives as the cause;

or at least when your own interest has too large a
proportion in your zeal.

3. When your zeal is more for the interest of your
adherents than for the church, and the common
cause of godliness and Christianity, and can be
content that some detriment to the whole may
further the interest of you and your adherents.

4. When your zeal tends toward hurt and cruelty and
would have God rather to glorify his justice by
some present notable judgment than his mercy by
patience and forgiving.

5. When your secret desire for fire from heaven (or
some destruction of the adversaries) is greater
than your desire and prayer for their conver-
sion. The sure mark of true zeal is zealous love: it
makes you love your neighbors and enemies more
fervently than others do.

6. When your zeal is out of proportion with your
understanding and your prudence and experience
are as much less than other people's, while your
zeal is greater. True zeal balances some equality of
light and heat.

7. When zeal is easily kept alive and hardly re-
strained, because it shows that selfish desire and
the devil are too much its friends. True zeal of

the spirit needs the fuel of all holy means and the bellows of meditation and prayer to kindle it. But carnal zeal will burn itself out without such endeavors.

8. When some forward teacher kindled zeal and not the sober preaching of the truth.

9. When zeal burns in the same soul where lust or wrath or pride or malice burns; and when it prospers at the same time that the love of God, and a heavenly mind and life, decay. The zeal of a sensualist, of a proud person, of a covetous person, of a self-conceited, empty person, can hardly be considered a spiritual zeal.

10. When zeal carries you away from the holy rule and pretends to come from a spirit that won't be tried by the scripture. Or when zeal drives you to use means that God forbids in his word, places you upon ways that the sealed law and testimony condemn. It can't be from God if it is against God's word.

By all these signs you may easily perceive how dividing zeal differs from genuine Christian zeal. The one is a zeal for some singular opinion; the other is a zeal for godliness and Christianity.

7. Separation Is Never God's Will

If you mark all the texts in the gospel, you will find that all the separation commanded in such cases is but one of the following two types: first, either the church casts out an impenitent sinner by the power of the keys to the kingdom; or, second, that members avoid familiarity with an impenitent sinner. And both these we would promote and in no way hinder.

But that the members should withdraw from the church because such sinful persons are not cast out of it, show us one text to prove it, if you can.

Let's peruse the texts that speak of our withdrawing from the wicked. First Corinthians 5 is expressly written to the whole church, as obliged "not to associate with anyone who calls themselves 'brother' or 'sister' who is sexually immoral, greedy, someone who worships false gods, an abusive person, a drunk, or a swindler. Don't even eat with anyone like this" (1 Cor 5:11). Now compare Titus 3:9-11: "Avoid stupid controversies, genealogies, and fights about the Law, because they are useless and worthless. After a first and second warning, have nothing more to do with a person who causes conflict, because you know that someone like this is twisted and sinful—so they condemn themselves." In brief, there is no other place of scripture that commands any more. The apostle never spoke a syllable to any Christian, telling them to separate from any one of all the churches. We can't imagine the Holy Spirit would have wholly omitted this if separation had been the will of God.

8. It Is Sinful
to Unchurch Persons

The sinfulness of unchurching persons, apart from Christ's due process, consists in the following:

1. It discards the laws of the great Lawgiver of the church and is thus contempt for God's authority, wisdom, and goodness by making ourselves greater or wiser or holier than God.

2. It is gross injustice to deprive people of such great privileges without any sufficient proof of their forfeiture.

3. It is an aggravated crime against them to denounce church tyranny in others but to be notoriously guilty of it themselves. What greater injustice and tyranny can there be than that a person's Christianity and church rights will be judged null, upon the censures and rumors of suspicious people, without any just proof or lawful trial? Why should it be in the power of everyone who uncharitably thinks evil of their neighbors, or believes reports against their innocence, to cast them out of God family and to unchristian and unchurch people arbitrarily at their pleasure?

Why is it okay for any person, overcome by passion but unreasonable enough, to say, "They are ignorant or profane," and then expect to have their neighbors excommunicated?

4. It makes all churches slippery and shadowy when a censorious person may unchurch them at their pleasure. What you say of others, another may say of you, and as justly expect to be believed.

5. It unavoidably brings in incurable divisions because there is no certain rule of justice with such persons. Therefore, they know not who are to be received to their communion and who are not. And the same person that one will think ought to be rejected and kept out, another will think is to be received.

Objection. But won't it be my sin if I communicate with persons I know to be wicked?

Answer. It will be your sin if you don't obey Christ (Matt 18:15) in admonishing them. But otherwise, if they are there without your fault, it is no more your sin to communicate with such people than it is to live and converse with fellow servants who are sinners. Those that come to Christ by faith, he will in no manner cast out or reject; so those that come to Christ by profession of faith, he won't have his ministers in any manner reject.

Coming to Christ, when he was personally on earth, signified following him as well as believing in him. So far as people will come, so far will they be received by Christ. If they will come toward him, he won't put them back. Many came to Christ, when he was on earth, whom he never repulsed, though he confounded others and caused grudges for entertaining them. Some came so far as to own Christ's name, and do miracles by it, that yet did not follow him; the apostles would have hindered them, but Christ reproved the apostles.

Directions to Pastors
to Prevent and Heal Division

◇

Oh my! Our preaching, praying, conference, and living tell the whole world that we are weak. How few are not either ignorant, or injudicious, or imprudent, or dull and lifeless, or dry and barren, or of stammering speech, in our ministerial work! And in so high a work, any one of these is a loathsome blemish.

If we are asked to defend our religion, or any necessary part thereof, how weakly and injudiciously it is usually done! In a word, our great divisions among ourselves, with our censures and usage of each other, tell the whole world not only that we are weak but that too many of us consider each other to be worse than weak—even intolerable.

And will we, by our weakness and faultiness, become the people's scandal and tempt them to undue separations? And when we have finished, be impatient with their weakness while we overlook our own?

When young and ungrounded Christians do, by their errors, pride, or passions, disturb the church's peace and order, it is the pastors that are usually first assaulted by their abuses and, therefore, are most impatient and exasperated against them. It would be well if we were so innocent ourselves, so that our consciences need not call us to inquire whether this is not partly the fruit of our own miscarriages. The church's peace lies chiefly in our hands, and if we miscarry, and won't understand instruction, nor bear admonition, nor do our parts, how little hope will be left of our tranquility. The body languishes when the physician is as bad as the disease.

On every side it is the pastors of the flocks that are accused by those of the adverse party as the chief offenders. One side says, "It is you that teach the people errors and put doubts into their minds and lead them into contempt of order and authority." The other side says, "It is you who proudly usurp authority that Christ never gave you and lord it over God's heritage and by your own invention lay snares before the people to divide them, which won't permit them to unite in their proper center and agree in basic simplicity."

And while each side is thus accused by the other, they have all the greater cause to suspect themselves because everyone seems to agree that it is the pastors who are principally at fault, though it is not agreed what the fault is nor which party of the pastors must bear the blame.

The following causes of the people's weakness and divisions are so openly manifest in too many pastors that they can't be concealed or excused:

1. There is so much ignorance in many that they are not able judiciously to edify the flocks nor to teach sound principles in a suitable manner and method to their hearers. Who can teach others that which they never learned themselves?

2. Too many don't understand the weaknesses of the ordinary person and therefore neither justly resolve their doubts nor answer their objections.

3. And how cold and unskillful are many in the application of that doctrine, which they have tolerably opened, and speak the truths of the living God without any affecting reverence or gravity. They talk drowsily about the evil of sin, the need of grace, the love of God in Jesus Christ, indeed about death and judgment, heaven and hell, as if it were their design to rock their hearers to sleep or make them believe that it is but a historical fiction they act and that nothing they say is to be believed! There is no need of any more forcible means to entice people to sin than to hear it preached against so coldly. We speak a few good words to the people in a reading tone, like a child that is saying a lesson, as if we don't believe it ourselves, and then we blame the people for not being edified by us. What can we expect from our drowsy and dry discourses but drowsiness in the hearers, if not contempt?

Our grave attire will go but a little way to maintain our reputation without some better testimony of our worth. An empty head; a stammering tongue; dry, dull, and disorderly preaching; senseless, cold, or confused praying; empty and frothy conversation will much abate the reverence of our persons.

If the church is ever healed of its wounds, it must be by the peaceable disposition of the pastors and people. If people ever come to a peaceable disposition, it must be by peaceable doctrine and principles—by a full and frequent explication of the nature, preeminence, and power of love. They must hear of it so much, and so long, until love is made their religion and becomes the natural heat and constitution of their whole beings. To promote this, the aged, experienced, and ripe kind of ministers and lay Christians must instill it into young Christians and scholars, that they may have nothing so common in their ears and studies as uniting love.

Let it also be observed that when pastors fall into parties, they always draw the people after them. Some take one side and some the other. If the officers divide, the soldiers will. If one side suppresses the other, it will nevertheless increase the schism, while the people will pity and plead for the party that is squashed down.

As to the immature, emptier sort of ministers, it is no wonder they don't understand what they never had opportunity to study or experience. But it is wished that they were so humble as to confess that they are yet immature and that time and long study is necessary to make them as wise as they think they are.

Oh that the ministers of Christ were once sensible, not here only but through the whole Christian world! What a plague is the conjunction of their ignorance, contentiousness, and dividing, selfish zeal to the church of Christ! And what they have done against the souls of people by violence and by heading parties, and by invoking heaven and hell and the salvation of their souls, upon the opinions that they never understood. By departing from simplicity to maintain their side and sanctity, by backbiting and reproaching others, whose persons perhaps they never met nor ever once soberly discoursed with face to face. Yet they make it their piety to revile by hearsay and judge in a cause they never heard nor understood.

If ever God shows mercy to his church, God will give them pastors after his own heart who will abound in light and love and lead the people into concord upon the ancient terms and make it their work to put this love-killing spirit to death. Death is at work through striving disputes, by dividing principles and practices, by reproaching others, by human cruelty, or by a religious, censorious cruelty, which does not kill nor strike people but drives them out of church and damns them.

Acknowledgment

◇

Decisions about what to include or omit were made while abridging a work that is based in sources from 1653 and 1670, when the dialect of Elizabethan English was spoken. We no longer speak this dialect, so the following principles guide the translation of archaic English in this further abridgment of Francis Asbury's selections in 1792.

First, scripture quotations are converted to the Common English Bible, which also influences the vocabulary and syntax of the text where biblical allusions are employed. Second, with occasional exceptions, the text is now gender inclusive. Third, archaic words and idioms are replaced with functional equivalents in present-day English. For example, few readers would know that a "jade," who plays "jadish tricks," is a worn-out old horse who is ill tempered. As another example, the word *livery* is replaced with "attire."

The structure and flow of the abridgment by Bishop Asbury is preserved, with the headings adjusted to fit with the selected excerpts as well as the translation principles.

This abridgment is based on Asbury's 1792 edition republished in 1849 by the Methodist Book Concern five years after the Northern and Southern Methodists divided over disagreements about slavery.

www.ingramcontent.com/pod-product-compliance
Lightning Source LLC
LaVergne TN
LVHW030636080426
835508LV00024B/3377